D1314094

MIDDLE DISTANCE

NONFICTION

W. W. NORTON & COMPANY
Independent Publishers Since 1923

MIDDLE DISTANCE

POEMS

STANLEY PLUMLY

For information about permission to reproduce selections from this book, write to
Permissions, W. W. Norton & Company, Inc., 500 Fifth Avenue, New York, NY 10110

For information about special discounts for bulk purchases, please contact
W. W. Norton Special Sales at specialsales@wwnorton.com or 800-233-4830

Manufacturing by Berryville Graphics
Book design by Abbate Design
Production manager: Anna Oler

Library of Congress Cataloging-in-Publication Data

Names: Plumly, Stanley, author.
Title: Middle distance : poems / Stanley Plumly.
Description: First edition. | New York : W. W. Norton & Company, [2020]
Identifiers: LCCN 2020010646 | ISBN 9781324006145 (hardcover) |
ISBN 9781324006152 (epub)
Subjects: LCGFT: Poetry.
Classification: LCC PS3566.L78 M53 2020 | DDC 811/.54—dc23
LC record available at https://lccn.loc.gov/2020010646

W. W. Norton & Company, Inc., 500 Fifth Avenue, New York, N.Y. 10110
www.wwnorton.com

W. W. Norton & Company Ltd., 15 Carlisle Street, London W1D 3BS

1 2 3 4 5 6 7 8 9 0

FOR JILL BIALOSKY

What matter if I live it all once more?

—W. B. YEATS,
"A DIALOGUE OF
SELF AND SOUL"

CONTENTS

PUBLISHER'S NOTE

Middle Distance was completed in February 2019 and is published posthumously. We are grateful to David Baker, Michael Collier, and, especially, Margaret Forian Plumly, for assisting in preparing and proofing the manuscript.

ACKNOWLEDGMENTS

T HESE WORKS first appeared in the following periodicals, to whose editors we extend our grateful acknowledgment: *The Account*, "Extremities"; *The American Poetry Review*, "Deathbed," "For Gerald Stern at Ninety-Two," "Planet," "Sycamore," "We Insomniacs," "Winter Evening"; *The Atlantic*, "Bluebird," "Waking"; *BODY*, "Blue Doves," "Germans"; *The Georgia Review*, "Night Pastorals," "Travel & Leisure"; *The Gettysburg Review*, "Crepuscular," "Doughboys," "Hawking," "The Ward"; *The Harvard Review*, "As You Leave the Room," "Sonnet"; *The Kenyon Review*, "Middle Distance," "Spring Photo," "White Rhino"; *The New England Review*, "Alzheimer's"; *The New Yorker*, "House"; *Poem-a-Day* (Academy of American Poets), "At Night"; *Poetry*, "Jesus Wept.," "The Winter Beach at Sanderling"; *Poetry Northwest*, "One of Ten." The "Place St.-Sulpice" and "Rue Férou" sections of "Travel & Leisure" appeared in *The Yale Review*. "With Weather" is a revised version of a poem that appeared in *How the Plains Indians Got Horses*, a chapbook from Best Cellar Press (1973).

MIDDLE DISTANCE

WHITE RHINO

The last of my kind, one of the last lovers of flowers
and the lawns of the northern grasses, and certainly
one of the few able to rub backsides with the baobab
and the century-nearing oak still surviving in the yard.

The trick is stone, to look like something broken
from a mountain, something so leftover so as not
to be alive, yet resemble in demeanor dream anger,
the kind that wakes you out of breath talking to yourself

in that language that starts in the belly and the bowel.
Old age is a disguise, the hard outside, the soft inside.
Even the plated armor is turning dust, then one foot
after the other, neuropathy my gravity, the footprint

larger, deeper. I hardly recognize myself except in
memory, except when the mind overwhelms the lonely
body. So I lumber on, part of me empty, part of me
filled with longing—I'm half-blind but see what I see,

the half sun on the hill. How long a life is too long,
as I take my time from here to there, the one world
dried-out distances, nose, horn, my great head lifted down,
the tonnage of my heart almost more than I can carry.

MIDDLE DISTANCE

Looking out at Constable's distances,
nothing I wanted to be, what I am.
He grows on you, Constable, so childish
at the beginning, toy farms, slow pastures,
the small trees bundled up as if for sale,
everything schooled out and diminished in
the direction of Salisbury—or
is it Dedham?—1804, thirty,
and already decades behind Turner.

History is easy. I could write all day
dropping names into the spaces between.
Most of C's best oils are on paper or
are drafts of pieces that get too finally
finished, even the very great ones
on which his fame, as we like to say, "rests."
Please look at his *A Cart with Two Horses*,
1814, workhorses of course, one
posed in profile, the other turned toward

the back of the painting, sold privately
cheaply, like most of his work. Millionaire
Turner evolves into near abstraction,
asking light to be sunlight purely, fire
from within nothing but what he calls a
landscape. Besides, he traveled, an antique
traveler in antique lands. But I love C's
local *Sketch of Tree Trunks, with a Figure*,
more oil on paper, seven years after *Horses*.

Constable is aging, failing.
He thinks I'm a cloud, a long white body
lying in the air over Hampstead, he thinks
clouds of storm shapes are bodies, like great elms.
I'm his anomaly, still thinning out.
Another day he sees me lying down
undulant in the middle distance, the
cloud come at last to earth as the earth is
part of the corn, the good ground under corn,

the painting piecemeal, the way he paints, so
that you have to stand at a real middle
distance just to see me. Turner wants me
to be *The Angel Standing in the Sun*,
apocalyptic in the afterlife,
though I prefer my body as a field
in which I live over again as flesh—
or is it flush?—against a stream, or of
the stream, as C also sees me, where a

boy on a barge on canvas is taking
a cloud-white horse to its destination
far downriver. And I am the water.
And the light on the water. And if it
is possible, having also been of
the plowed and planted and replanted earth,
I am the sky domed over the boat boy's
possible future, when he then arrives
and puts to work all that really matters.

PLANET

There is the thought that when you go you take it all with you,
whatever all is: dying as either an ontological condition
of past-caring or a heartsick feeling that none of it mattered,
not the friend forgotten nor the friend denied,
not the child that didn't happen
nor the years lost nor the day you walked away,
not the century since nor the days-on-end of starting out the day,
not the thinking and rethinking what you thought—
now that your body is no longer yours nor even a body
in death's fantasy but a look-alike of makeup and sweet fluids,
lifted as a soul by several plaited ropes and planted
in the pastoral if alien green ground, soon to be, in the image
of Walt Whitman, a leaf of grass, lilac, or budding apple tree,
or even better, "the resurrection of the wheat."

When I was twelve, when all of us were there,
I watched a bawling steer, locked in the vise of a large steel collar,
receive—between its wide black eyes—at least one blow
of one sledgehammer, if only to stun it
and allow it to be dragged and strung up by its length
where another boy—maybe high school or older—slit its throat
with the half-moon of a knife, to let the blood spout out,
the animal still alive before the next in line.
Then, in the spring, Mary Neal, the one true angel in the class,
whose beauty was enough, could not transcend the polio around her,
which rose like heavy water inside her,
so that on our visits all we could see was her loyal head
emerging from the white enamel breathing of the lung,
the rearview mirror fixed in such a way she didn't have to look at us.

For too many years I dreamed of her or someone like her
at the far end of a platform or at a window on a train
slowly coming in, her face half profiled in the late evening sunlight
the way, in the way of recurring dreams, we fall in love.
The mistake would be, in real life, to try to meet that train,
to be standing there, waiting: and then a day it happens,
and you can see in the light blue marbling of her eyes how this
was meant to be, except it wasn't, it was dreaming of another kind,
once the closing dark has subtracted everything—
was she beautiful, lying there, nineteen fifty-one,
dying in ways that were invisible?—
and what is this loneliness we long for in that someone
no one else can be, who lives or dies, depending,
but who was there, whatever the moment was?

SYCAMORE

If you couldn't have an elm-lined walk,
you might have one of these for show-and-tell,
with Mrs. Allen standing at the back end
of the class, who meant for us to hold up
one example of a leaf and talk the best
we could in front of every other stumbling
second-grader, whose usual was scarlet maple,
golden oak, or some hybrid color heart-shaped
half-spotted kind of thing, half-wet or fading
as the storyteller wandered through the history
of how he or she got here safely with it. Mine,
from the front lawn, was hardly any better,
since it covered more than twice my opened fingers,
palmate on my palm, and was turning toward
its dry and pockmarked end, like my now vein-heavy
hands, which, when the nurses try for blood,
are better than the arms. As I remember,
these thousand years ago, I held it from my body
as if while I was talking it had died and my story
was an elegy of time, the season passing, winter
coming on. Of course, this is a lie: I was silent
and stood there in my cylinder of silence like
the tree the leaf had fallen from, until the teacher,
in her mercy, told me to sit down, the way
I'm sitting now, typing. Nothing ever dies,
says the science of mortality—it's all chemistry
and change from one form to another. I was dying
holding on to dear life with a dead leaf that was
changing even further in the endless moment
that morning, curling, still alive, within my hand.

WINTER EVENING

Give it another month from now, though why wait
on ceremony, the winter light this early late November
evening the soft blue bruise of where the heart has
thinned the blood—and cold, so cold, the kind of clarity
a star will clarify before the sky is full of them, the blue
gone for good. Someone asked me earlier today about
how the past is people, which I took to mean a memory,
a question that had more to do with why we remember
who we remember, right down to the coloration in an eye,
probably blue, since brown is too common and any darker
the absent color of midnight and any lighter only daylight.

Children cover their eyes in order to become invisible,
as later they disappear into their eyes, the way sunlight
leaves and enters and within the imagination takes on
meaning, say blue in all its variety and depth, which, like
beauty, is in the blue eye of the beholder. Though I wonder.
Love is a kind of beauty, the moment its own memory
in the eye of the lover looking back at you, her blue eyes
the blue of right before sunset, blue filling the fire
still in the air, blue lingering, blue fading, blue closing,
then first thing in the morning opening blue again,
blue all the longer hours, until the dream end of the day.

Why were we alive? Radical Harry Berger for one, who, after
a Rockefeller month and two days after nine/eleven can't take
Villa Serbelloni anymore and, warned, uses up his pre-dawn free
car ride to the Milan airport only to be told two weeks and no
sooner for international air space to be cleared—so there I am
waiting at the Bellagio boat dock to take Harry, whom I love, to
lunch in order to assuage, as we say, his anger. It has taken him all
morning, early afternoon to retrace his various steps, on his own
thin dime, by train and ferry, back. Luggage and all.

Bellagio is too beautiful,
Lake Como too beautiful,
lovely Bellagio, according to
Shelley, "the pearl of the lake."
Proletariat Harry, Socialist
Harry misses the seal-gray,
sealed-off fog of Northern
California rolling into his
Pacific-facing windows at
home; misses the wine, the
exotic salads, the elevated
attitudes of the ordinary;
misses his worktable, his
lonely meals, his cat, his
passionate prose about art,
which can only be written
among the surround of his
thousands of books smiling
down at him hard at his desk.

Karlův Most, for another, or if you're just passing over the Vltava
River, the Charles Bridge, the Bridge of Saints, the bridge at night
in which ghosts rise from the water in the guise of fog, and if
it's late enough and only a few of us, whether tourists or leftover
musicians, the saint you're standing under will look straight
at you and see into your heart. Saint Francis, for example, the
youngest, 1855, whose head is blessed by small songbirds during
the day and wears them as a crown, in the dusk and dark must be
blessed instead with mist. He looks down at me, and I look down,
look through the moving luminous air spread over the water, and
see a woman I loved dead in the river, floating for a moment in
the bridge light cast like a hand of benediction.

Bridges are dangerous, they cross
the powers of the pull of the earth
as if these were mere temptations
to join dark water or the deep path
that have all along been waiting
if only when we recognize what
they are for what they are. When
Deborah jumped, for instance, she
must have thought what was under
her was water willing to love her
the way she was loved by so many.
Suicide is about the imagination.
It's a decision based on evidence.

Place St.-Sulpice, the square, in the twenties, about which
Hemingway writes that if "you came out of the Luxembourg you
could walk" to "down the narrow rue Férou," yet adds that "there
were still no restaurants, only the quiet square with its benches
and trees. There was a fountain with lions, and pigeons walked
on the pavement and perched on the statues of the bishops. There
was the church and there were shops selling religious objects
and vestments on the north side. . . ." When I was there, in the
eighties, St.-Sulpice was still quiet, with benches and large plane
trees and pigeons on the heads of the bishop statues and the
heads of the lions, yet there were no shops to speak of though
there were restaurants, at least one, where I would sit away the
afternoon nursing a slow wine and slower coffee, then once in
a while walk over to pet the noses of the lions, which resemble,
almost to scale, the lions in front of the New York City Public
Library on Fifth Avenue.

Rue Férou, one of the loveliest small
streets in Paris, perfect as a lane between
the grand church and the grander gardens.
At night, the City of Light is defined in
sum by this square and its leonine silences,
save for the waterfall of the fountain. In
the autumn, the best time, the big sycamore-
size leaves drift down everywhere—onto
the slate slabs and cobblestones of the square,
onto the glass tables with their plates
of breads and cheeses and cheap white wine,
onto the heads and bodies of the bishops
and the lions—then the wind kicks up.
I'd have walked the late afternoon through
the well-ordered, well-kept deep green
gardens, have found a table near the front

of where the fountain was, and watched
the evening turn blue and dark and darker.
No one died, nor was ever going to die.

———

Like lying on a bench in an intimate summer space below the Pont
Neuf, at an edge of the Île de la Cité, looking up, in one direction,
at the head half of the statue of Henri Quatre and in another
direction at pooled water and large gray roots and branches: an
almost secret place Hemingway locates as "a point like the sharp
bow of a ship," where "there was a small park at the water's edge
with fine chestnut trees, some huge and spreading, and in the
currents and back waters that the Seine made flowing past . . .
excellent places to fish." He describes the fish as "dace-like"—
goujon—"plump and sweet-fleshed with a finer flavor than fresh
sardines," and especially delicious when fried whole. We're talking
thirty years ago for me and nearly a century for Hemingway, yet
the fishermen, with their cane poles and "light gear," were still
there, and, I hope, there now, like the trees.

That feeling, lying there, looking up and out,
coffeed-up yet ready to fall asleep—I think
I fell deeply and drifted in the dream itself
of lying there, like those childhood naps
in which we see ourselves sleeping, afraid
someone will wake us. Someone always does.
My weakness, generally, is the quiet seduction
of withdrawal, to hide out within myself,
to disappear. Everything inside me sort of
shuts down or seems to, except the eyes,
which take on a different register, and here

in the laze of a summer afternoon with nowhere
to go, nothing to do, and no one to see, and seems
to find a higher intensity, as if seeing through
something more than air—like color in the light
brighter, sleeping altogether of another order.

———

Each weekday morning at around nine I'd walk over to where
Randolph Road runs into Clifton Gardens and pick up the #47
and bus up to Rosslyn Hill Road at Pond Street in Hampstead, a
ride of about a half an hour or so. In winter a little longer. Pond is
a wind-swept steep descent and steeper climb leading to and from
East Heath Road, where, on my way to the Keats House, I'd stop
off at a local bakery for a take-out coffee and sweet roll. Pond is
also the street Keats walks down, at eleven at night, February 3,
1820, without his great coat. He's coached up to Hampstead from
London proper, on some of the same route as my morning trips.
Pond Street, with its icy wind, deep dive, and small reservoir
at the bottom, proves to be the fateful walk leading to his first
hemorrhage, his "death warrant."

The Michelin writes that "Hampstead Heath
was the common of Hampstead Manor in
Charles II's reign, an area where laundresses
laid out washing to bleach"—Common, with
a capital because of its size as a woodland,
cropland, pasture, and open walking park,
larger than Hyde or Regent's Park, the place
where Keats meets Coleridge for the one
and only time, on an April Sunday: "There
is death in that hand," Coleridge

would write, though at the time the subject
was nightingales, which kept the Great Ruin
awake and which greeted Keats each evening
singing within the enclosure of the Wentworth
gardens: invisible, their hearts in their throats.

———

Of ruins, Henry James writes that "Beauty is no compensation
for the loss, only making it more poignant. Enough beauty of
climate hangs over . . . Roman cottages and farm-houses—beauty
of light, of atmosphere and of vegetation; but their charm for the
maker-out of the stories in things is the way the golden air shows
off their desolation." Where I grew up in Ohio a farmhouse
was likely not to last longer than a lifetime, unless it was built
of brick or stone, and even then it required dedication. The red
brick walls of ours were already pockmarked with holes by the
time we moved in the year after the world war, as if they had
survived the war, when it was only age and weather, the drilling
of rain and snow.

As a child I would wake up listening
to the wind finding the indentations,
whistling the losses. The cold air, at
two or three in the morning, was iron,
though the evening before, especially
autumn, could be warm and golden
against the dying leaves. Winter I
could write my name in the ice on
the window at the head of my bed.
Why were we alive? To remember,
for one thing, and to forget. Walking

the cracked stone sidewalk along
the Tiber, its pale green color igniting
the sun, its smooth lazy gliding surface
bearing the burden of one big leaf
after another, even as early as summer,
from row after row of the distances
drawn along the banks by plane trees—
leaves larger than your praying hands—
that day breathing that air all afternoon.

———

I'm going to invent Venice, though the question divides between
the Stato da Màr and the Stato da Tera, islands or mainland, or
the fact that the difference makes no difference. For my mother,
for whom imagination is everything, it doesn't, as she looks down
at a map of the Veneto and all the names she can't pronounce nor
even really see through the mask of her macular degeneration.
So I'm focusing and making Venice up for her—not as City of the
Dead but City of the Afterlife, soul to soul, spirit to spirit, and
so on. So forget Ezra Pound buried above ground-level on the
island of San Michele, forget the sinking marble palaces along
the byways and lagoons, ignore the little life under your feet,
think instead of Longfellow's "white swan of cities," remember
woefully-Belmont-County-Ohio-born (my county) William Dean
Howells' comment that what "summer-delight of other lands
could match the beauty of the first Venetian snow-fall which I
saw," listen to Dickens "looking down upon the Grand Canal and
away, beyond, to where the sun went down to-night in a blaze." I
watched my mother die, I sat beside her holding her hand to the
sound of the machine breathing for her; I permitted it, and now at
the age she passed I have permission.

Turner's watercolors, Whistler's nocturnes . . .
That's how my mother sees in general now,
the red wash of sunrise, the watery blue mist
of night lit down the alleyways of the canals
with Christ's candles or pagan moonlight,
depending on her mood and how much work
I can manage detailing architecture and bridges,
then in daylight the Piazza San Marco with its
clock tower and basilica and panoramic floor
and small medieval people dressed alive,
strolling, gathering, meeting the secret loved one.
My mother wants to meet, I think, the loved
one or someone she remembers now forgotten.
I can't imagine who he is except the longing.

———

Three hundred and sixty square granite miles, two roads or
trackways, east-west, northeast-southwest, rising a thousand feet
at Two Bridges, two thousand feet at the highest tors, among a
landscape of wooded valleys, fast cold streams, rough fields, small
farms, and a few rustic villages, and everywhere leftover tin-
mine ponies, Blackfaced Scottish sheep, Galloways and Highland
cattle, ravens, kestrels, buzzards, and bogs that swallow whole the
animal. This is Dartmoor, home of the hound of the Baskervilles.
This is stone-mass risen from stone-back of the sea, this is
Chagford, Haytor Rocks, Princetown Prison, and Wistman's
Wood. For all the space, you cannot park your car except where
marked, while even walking it's best to parallel the road. Lost is
lost here. The winds arrive from the ocean, nothing but distance
to slow them: they chill the heart right down to the chill ground.

Nature is everything we aren't,
plus the old tin mines, the wells,
and the cairns meant to memorialize
humanity and its sad face looking
out over the desolation, over the
sheep wandering the road, the pony
capsized in quicksand, the hawk
circling a kill. The rain is sideways
with the wind, stunting and slanting
odd places on the landscape like the
outcrop of the primal lichened oaks
of Wistman's Wood. I stood on one
of its boulders to take a picture of
the view, which was nothing but
empty moorland yet beautiful in
its emptiness, rendered down to
only what it was. The cutting wind
made me cry, which itself was full
of tears. I could hear a curlew or
a miner's gull blown in from the sea,
the light the flat tin silver of the mines.

———

In the middle of his life Turner paints a watercolor of water with
three boats in *Boats at Sea*, none of which realities are present.
The sea is yellowy fog the color, width, and depth of paper,
22.2 x 28 cm; the boats are three small brush marks, one bold
and black, one—on the viewer's left—pale red, like kissed lipstick,
and one behind these two, smaller and also black. What are we
looking at from this master of the color wheel and "ships at sea,"
this master of the sun pouring through the canvas, this artist of
the mist, this seer who turns stone into the ethereal, this man

who burns away appearances? This artist, writes Hazlitt, "delights
to go back to the first chaos of the world. . . . All is 'without form
and void.' Some one said of his landscapes that they were *pictures
of nothing and very like.*"

What is very like nothing—is void nothing?
Turner was not very good at painting people,
so they become either wraithlike or absent.
He loves boats, he loves looking at Venice
from the sea, he loves distance, disappearance,
the velocities of color moving at the speed
of light—he's an arsonist of what he sees.
He loves his father. Is a picture of the ocean
a landscape, does a ship make a pastoral?
Here's *The Great Western Railway* Firefly
coming at you—*Rain, Steam and Speed*—
is this the first industrial pastoral, with
an iron rail bridge spanning the Thames
at Maidenhead? Thirty years on, Whitman
will celebrate a "Locomotive in Winter"
passing through snow and "buffeting gusts
of wind," and his "Fierce-throated beauty!"
of a train is poetry no less a pastoral,
no less powerful than the B&O engines
that passed and ever so much shook
our house each day going where? My
mother hated them, but paint them,
write them, they move while staying
still. Turner's train, in fact, almost
disappears into its generated painted
rain and steam—it's on a wall at the
Tate; Whitman's on a page pressed like
an autumn leaf. At night, asleep, I heard
them, pushing ahead the dark darker.

A landscape you can walk into, though on the condition you're willing to dissemble what you are into a snow of paint in a storm of heavy muted color, where the body of the one becomes the body of the whole, the young man in the red shirt leaning over the canal lock part of the lock. Robert Lowell writes of the painter that "in his sketches more finished than his oils, / sketches made *after* he did those masterpieces, / Constable can make us *see* the breeze . . ." Is this insecurity or vision—still not seeing enough into the plasma of the thing, oil sketch after sketch, before and after the painting he will hang? Then the late work gothic in its drafting of near night, no more noon self-referencing of building or guiding a workboat down the Stour, no more perfection of Willy Lott's sweet cottage, only the breakdown of a leaping horse. Yet even in the finished version all of it in pieces.

The Englishness of his trees, the risk
of being a boy as a character, the far-off
seeing of depths of fields—I see myself
drinking from the stream, the dog trying
to warn me the sheep are wandering
toward *The Cornfield*, the farmer at the
broken gate making his judgment: I love
this 1826 biblical plot of painting of
innocence, which I take at my own leisure,
real hearts in real ground, real wheat. In
Constable we live as we lived, loved within
what he called "the *chiaroscuro* of nature."
It's the warmth, the all-embracing texture
of the sheer application of the paint itself
that loves us, the point of each brushstroke

palpable at once in two worlds: his at the
Dedham/Bergholt/Hampstead source,
ours in our simply standing there looking
at the art for as long as ever in our eyes.
He says, in an elegiac moment, that our
hearts are in the sky, meaning his cumulo-
nimbus clouds, meaning Maria is dying.
He even tries, in the weather over Hampstead
and those storm days at the beach, at Brighton,
to paint, at the end of everything, real rain.

HAWKING

The wind down from the barely Catoctin Mountains
that are only high enough in weather to help cause it,
the red-tail riding in on one of the skyways, the same
hawk, I think, that spread its shadow on the window
and the one I saw catch a crow midair and break it;
otherwise, some days nothing but the rain, other days
the crossfire of the sun. I had a rifle when I was ten
whose lonely bullet would travel the visible length
of light just far enough to miss what it looked for—
it was a .22 caliber and required more than sight to hit
what it aimed at, which was never, since every missed
gunshot goes somewhere and could still be traveling
toward whatever life is flying or caged among dead
branches or gathered in small numbers in leafy corners:
it would be silent as a thought within a mind of its own
and would be and in all ways moving at all deliberate
speed, trailing the least expected, at all hours, even
heading toward a reader reading under glass,
who's looking up at us, right now, in innocence,
thinking of something else: for sure it will be following
the long elliptic of the way things can come back to you,
come home, here in the heart, back into the gun . . .

BLUE DOVES

I remember a day in Houston, in the death
throes of summer, a young man nailing
a live swan to a tree in the posture
of the Christ in an argument with beauty.
There was a picture in the paper, front
page, as if this news was the end of cruelty.

This morning mourning doves rhyming
their hearts out, while later on this evening
they'll sing even deeper in their melancholy,
which is an o-vowel sound we sometimes hear
in our sadness as an elegy. Sometimes a sound
all afternoon as well, right on through the cruel

hours of the heat building toward the middle
of the night, when no one can get to sleep.

SPRING PHOTO

It isn't so much the capture of snow falling and melting
all at once in the background, streaking as if on a window,
like little souls passing—not so much the poetry of evocation
as the fact of the fragment of a branch and the snowfall gathered
along it, plus the smaller, delicate branches shooting off it,
one of which, in the studied foreground, is holding, in ascending
order, a tufted titmouse, a female cardinal, and a white-throated
sparrow, though the caption lists the three of them in reverse,
which has a point, since the titmouse weighs less and is last
and the sparrow is the marker, meaning it likely landed first,
while the winter-feathered, rose-tinted cardinal is perfect in the
middle, otherwise the balance would be off, the branch unsafe,
the patience of the picture-taker tested, who's been waiting
in the cold who knows how long or happened on a lucky shot.

SONNET

Like a light coastal rain, with its sadness,
the windshield spotted with it, wiped away,
the wipers like a metronome, an hour maybe,
my sister and I waiting in the truck, the motor
running to keep us company, and night coming
on at any minute . . . He'd say he'd be a minute,
and knowing was enough, the streetlights already
bright among the black slick coiling of the air
and the counting of headlights passing through
the cab and the wet singing of the tires against
the wetter pavement and—what else?—people
on the street, sometimes looking in or looking
straight ahead, red neon signing on, signing off,
the great evening all around us darker, tighter.

DOUGHBOYS

Naturally, as you age your past accumulates as old memory,
the landscapes and the ruins that Freud, for one, understood
as archaeology, remembered or refused, and that survive
like bones or pottery or outlines of foundations of imaginary
cities, or like souls that to one degree or other still live a life
inside you and whose number seems enormous, like a town,
to whom you'd like to say, one soul at a time, I'm sorry that
in my heart back then I killed you, wished you away, closed
my eyes and, for that moment, you were gone—Harry Sullen-
burger, for one, my mother's mother's sad second husband,

who, like her first, was a kind of homegrown German,
and who, as if to compensate, volunteered for Wilson's War,
and survived because his stature was equal to John Keats,
the swarm of the machine-gun fire strafing above his head
buried in the trenches—Harry the troglodyte, grounded
in a grave, who would hold his helmet up on the end
of his bayonet to check, on the hour, death's weather—Harry
the shell-shocked veteran, home not soon enough, his voice
like a brick or brick dust from the gas, smoking his King Edwards,
piled into his chair, his bare trench feet well short of the floor—

and Harry the janitor, four in the afternoon, trudging from French
Oil, his long bib overalls rolled up like a boy's, so that after school,
when I see him, I cross to the other side, though I hear
in the mythic air the cock crow thrice, and this happens more
than once, as when he dies, the way my father dies, drinking,
I cross the street again—Harry invisible, the citizen of sorrow—
Harry in his fifties, listening to *The Shadow* on the full-sized Philco,
where I'm lying on the floor listening too, on one side of him

the stand-up glass ashtray, filled with his cigar stubs,
on the other a lurid stack of years of *True Detectives*—Harry

talking through the talking on the radio, mumbling through booze—
Gassed, the painting by Singer Sargent, in which a blinded squad
of Wilfred Owen infantry are moving in a line in a direction
to nowhere, the remainder of the troop lying in positions of
exhaustion and surrender, though it's the texture of the uniforms,
the drying blood, the sallow toxic color of the sky, all of it in browns
of excrement applied with a sable brush and palette knife,
that is the real study here—John Singer Sargent, still famous
for imperially posed women, their several children, in settings
of due elegance, arranged like flowers in classic-colored still lifes.

GERMANS

There are eleven of them. Why I remember the exact number
is uncertain, perhaps because it's enough to field a football
team. They arrive by train, a short sixty-mile ride west from
Washington, D.C., to Winchester, Virginia, an old Civil War
town that has the distinction of having been exchanged, North
and South, more than seventy times, 1861–1865. They're dressed
in army prison khaki green, black boots, and are marched like
soldiers—which they are—right through the center of town,
right from the station past the Frederick County Courthouse and
the Great Red Wooden Apple on its front lawn, past the Greco-
Roman-inspired architecture of the Public Library, and on out to
the P. W. Plumly Lumber Corporation sawmill. To say they march
is probably an exaggeration of their very formal walking, whose
stride is nevertheless very military. It's a parade, maybe 9:00 or
so in the morning, May, as I remember, 1944, my father, with his
holstered .22 pistol, at the head of the local National Guard that is
escorting them to the Quonset-hut quarters my grandfather has
had specially built for them.

In spite of the hour, there are lots of spectators along the sidelines,
mostly mothers and small children, plus a few towny dignitaries,
even Senator Harry Byrd (who has sponsored their arrival) and P.
W. and some employees, though, now that I think about it, they're
all likely waiting for the Germans at the other end. It's rained
earlier, so the red brick streets are slick and the procession slower
than it might be. That way you really get to look at them, enemy
and alien, a whiter race, having arrived, as if from outer space,
from a far-off foreign war. I'm still not in school, since there's no
kindergarten; I have plenty of time and freedom to take things in,
whether or not I understand them.

My father has complained for some time that he's shorthanded
for the out-in-the-field jobs, a consequence, by now, of more
than three years of the American participation in the war.
Lumberjacking, even in the relatively new-growth parts of the
Shenandoah, is tough, young work. The Shenandoah is protected
property, state and federal, but in these war years you can lease
heavily forested areas for selective harvest. My grandfather
also owns farmland just at the edge of the city, which he turns
into apple orchards. So on the one hand, he's in the business
of bringing down trees—big hardwoods—and, on the other,
planting trees for cultivation. (The economy for him, and for
many American businessmen, is the war; and still will be well
after the war.) My grandfather, in the best sense, then, is a farmer
of trees. In good weather, as I remember, we camp out in the Blue
Ridge for two or more days at a time, though I usually don't last
the third night. It's the cold more than anything, the thick damp
cold that settles in from the thickness of the leaves. It falls like
breaths of rain.

The few men my father normally works with are all older: poor,
white, heavy smokers, with drawn, masklike faces, and bodies
that seem, from forever, bone-tired. They're leftovers—men too
old or out of sorts to volunteer or get drafted. My young father
is the straw boss. The Germans are here to fill out the workforce.
They don't seem to mind their mission, which is essentially forced
labor: for them it's a kind of freedom—from the war, from prison,
from soldiering, from fighting, from death, and from filth, poor
food, and, what I would imagine to be if I were older, the noises of
death and death's silences.

It turns out that as the war in Europe seems to be either building
or winding down or simply exhausting itself—though who can
tell with the ongoing prevalence of those button-size red coupons

and white lard-like butter substitutes and rag-and-paper drives and endless ads for war bonds—it turns out that we have as many as five hundred internment camps here in America, mostly populated by Germans. These camps are everywhere, including farm country as well as just outside major cities. The 1929 Geneva Convention stipulates that war captives must be "housed safely and fed well"—a "Geneva holiday" it's called. There are enough POWs nationwide to make a fair-size international city: 371,000 Germans, 51,000 Italians, and 5,500 Japanese. Occasionally prisoners are "released" out into the community to fill in for the absent military-age population, which is how my grandfather secures his eleven Germans. Virginia's senior senator Byrd is a friend, and as a gesture of thanks for my grandfather's financial support against Roosevelt and the Democrats as well as his war contribution (for one, the manufacture of Piper airplane propellers), Byrd manages to requisition these prisoner soldier-officers for whatever work my grandfather's lumber business needs doing—from labor at the sawmill to planting apple trees to, more importantly, cutting down hardwoods. The Germans are already in Virginia, in a camp outside Washington.

Lumber camp will be a camp of an altogether other kind. Mostly, I think, it has to do with focus and clarity. It's all and only about the trees and the men—ten, twelve hours a day over, say, a three-day period, usually middle of the week. Other than the work, it's like camping out, at least for me it is, whenever my father lets me tag along. I won't be in school until I'm six and the war over, so it's an experience well beyond the task at hand. It's an other-planetary German experience.

Though it's the big trees that matter most. From my five-year-old perspective, looking up through an oak's muscular branching, the older regular loggers are, too much of the time, men who seem diminished next to what they are trying to bring down. For me the largest of the trees loom like—what?—gods, though that's a concept I have no idea of, only an impression of something wholly surpassing, like pictures of great animals in books: mystical oaks and spread-out, big-leaved maples and shagbark hickories among the most prized. On clear days, summer and fall, the broken sunlight falling through the oak and maple and hickory branches makes for a deeper, higher stillness, and an even greater stillness if you can stand alone next to one and look straight up through the pieces of the green and blue canopy. It turns you around, just standing there, with your head back, so that you have to lean against the tree's rough body in order to keep your balance. Trees, by themselves, are grand enough, but in vast numbers on the side of a mountain they take on a wild, other life. But it seems to me, in this moment, I'm the only one who thinks so. This is business and the task is too difficult to think much at all. The Germans, unlike the men my father has generally had to work with, seem to be a natural fit for the scale and labor of the trees, if only because they're happy to be anywhere outside the stockade.

—————

The Germans seem to a child to be as strong and stubborn as the trees—lean, straight, hard as the wood just under the bark. Then again, their blondish heads look square to me, as if their minds have corners. Out on the job in the Shenandoah, the Germans pay no attention, which is easy all around, since my own job is to be sort of gone, to hang at the near peripheries. I am, therefore, neither seen nor heard, except when I'm not. It's not natural to be completely quiet, though quiet is how you hear what's really going on—nature, Germans, or otherwise. I guess I spend as much time watching the birds and squirrels and the occasional surprised deer as I do witnessing the work. The songbirds and the crows chatter and caw throughout the day and fly in and out of the shadows as if on business, which, I suppose, they are on. The squirrels sort of chatter too and zip electric from place to place as if wired—in a few years I'll try to shoot them with small-bore bullets and never hit one.

There are probably black bears, but there are too many of us for the curious. This may not be the wild exactly, the distant strange world you see in books and at the movies, but it's natural, right along the edges of where people live. And there are ruins, natural ruins, fallen dead trees and parts of trees all mixed up together, limbs crossed over, trunks rotted and split open, root and branch in pieces. The universally gray tree parts just lie there, like ghosts of themselves, between here and the invisible. Most of the parts will in no time turn into splinter and dust. Sometimes the look of an area of debris is like a book picture of a beached shipwreck or an old building whose rotted wooden interiors have collapsed—it's hard for me not to want the picture to look like something else. The loggers move the debris if it's in the way or cut it up for firewood if it's dry and there's not too much of it or simply work around it.

It's different at the sawmill, where the huts are and where the Germans work in twos and threes on small jobs. I keep my distance there as well, but not too far. They're exotic and fun to watch; we get used to one another. If they're dangerous they hide it behind their stoicism or a humor that doesn't translate, which is to say they go their own way or if they do become engaged with me they sort of laugh, sort of smile, or otherwise relax their tight faces as if in spite of themselves. Perhaps they see me as a kind of mascot. Looking back, the situation is absurd. I must be as exotic to them as they are to me, or else I remind them of home. They have, more or less, the freedom of the mill and, later on, the greater freedom of the woods. As for escape, where would they go that would be any better, and why would they go, since, as everyone says, the almost-over war is far away and Hitler is doomed. *Hitler* is the word used instead of the word *war* more often than not.

Around me they show, as my mother would call it, strict manners, but they're not cold. They treat me with a certain trepidation and curiosity; I treat them with a certain fascination. We both speak a kind of Dutch English. Before they arrived I hung around the mill and mill's offices like a fantasy spy, keeping watch on the help at the big machines slowly rendering the raw wood into something useful or checking up on the small talk of the secretaries, busy with typing or filling orders. Compared to the regulars—in the yard or in the office—these Germans move at a different speed, so, of course, to me they add something spectacular, as if they're playing at the work. I'm probably the only one who thinks so. Those in charge and those who are generally adults seem to tense around them, as if they expect to be challenged or suddenly treated to violence.

The Germans, as if naturally, learn the ear-splitting and dangerous ripsaw jobs of the mill with ease, jobs that involve lifting the logs by small crane onto a great table, then unchaining them between vises and making sure they run true into the teeth of the huge saw-wheel that turns like a wheel of fire. First the bark is trimmed, then the naked logs themselves are run back and forth and sized into lumber. The whining of the ripsaw machine is an ear-killing sound—its high-scream octave drives straight to the heart. To save their hearing, the men wear plugs. I simply hold my hands over my ears and stand at a distance, in awe. The resonant smell, too, has power—it's almost like a drug on the air the way the heartwood odor carries and dominates and makes you cough to clear your nose and throat. It's the kind of odor you never lose a sense of.

The war, at this point, is wearing out everyone's patience. My father, at twenty-eight, is in charge here at home, whatever that means. I think what it means is that he's responsible for the Germans' and the mill Virginians' full day of work. He's at a soldier's age. He's, in fact, a contemporary of the prisoners he's responsible for. And these soldiers know who I am. I think they must see in me something of normalcy. And since there is no kindergarten—a German word—they and their schedule represent for me a kind of school. I'm around sometimes in the morning, sometimes the afternoon, breakfast or lunch. What I remember most about breaking bread with them is that they not only work hard but eat hard. They eat tremendous amounts of cheese and eggs and pour milk from heavy dairy containers that come directly from the farm, my grandfather's farm, where the apple trees are. The containers are cold, metal cold; milk is the Germans' manna from heaven—they often lift the containers to show off and drink the fresh chilled milk flush.

My lasting eating impression is that they take in their food primarily with their hands, very washed hands. They eat rapidly and completely. This all makes sense to me. I envy them their permission to eat with their hands. To be fair, much of their food is intended to be eaten with their fingers—chicken, corn-on-the-cob, boiled potatoes, raw vegetables, apples, and, of course, fresh bread, which they dip into milk. I imagine that some of what war is is eating with your hands and eating fast. There are worktables in the middle of their two Quonset spaces, where my father joins me in one of the huts in our sometimes lunch with them. More times than not the Germans prefer holding their plates on their laps sitting on cots or folding chairs. The fresh milk is the best I've ever tasted.

Sleep is another thing: those mornings that I follow with my father on a work detail out into the woods the Germans seem to have slept with the same hard sense of their ultimate mealtime purposes, as if they were eating sleep. The long hot work hours are part of it; the strict timeframes of the daily schedule are another part; the clarity of their situation is another—their responsibilities are pure. They haven't lasted long as apple pickers, planters, or orchard mowers. But they're a natural for loggers. Their skills on the big table saws and their abilities as a working group have soon moved them to the mill or transported them out among the Shenandoah's shadows, which is where I first notice what strikes me as their unusual whiteness, their mental intensity, their inherent suggestion of superiority, even if—as I would read years later—"they were in the forced service of their captors."

They are, after all, Nazis, a self-proclaimed race apart. They have doubtless killed Americans, yes, but also all kinds of people, including children. They have, as representatives, murdered people in their sleep—at least as I imagine. I will be close to seven or eight and the Germans will be long gone before I see the first Pathé half-time newsreel pictures of the concentration camps, let alone the forties war movies in which allies are tortured, shot down in cold blood, or sent to the camps or—if lucky in the happier films—successful in making their way out of a capture to safety. (*Casablanca* is the preternatural example of kiss-and-run escape.) Yet, in this moment, in this spring and summer of 1944, at the mill or out in the woods, this sense of this enemy as the absolute enemy, this sense of these particular men as evil fades in close company. They are, at worst, a rumor to me; at best, living, very-present presences.

Who knows what wounded and disabled veterans now home, now here in Winchester, for the rest of their altered lives, think . . .

But even the barky tone of the Germans' spoken language— its guttural, blunt-edged, consonantal sounds—strikes me as familiar, human, like someone who is constantly trying to clear his throat. *Ich, kartoffel, milch, baum*. In the woods, among the echo-chamber stands of trees, their rough dark voices reclarify the silences and give the summer warmth of the trees a ringing feel of abruptness, all business. These Germans don't seem to me to be bad men, yet by their being here they also imply an ability to reduce the world around them to function, to something they can stand against, even dominate, engineer into submission. I'm a child, an American, so I don't qualify as important enough to worry the final questions of their future or the future of the war. Insofar as I'm a concern, I'm not; their field of vision begins at about a foot or two above my head. Americans, generally, here at home, seem to be beyond their bother. The trees, though, are the perfect challenge, which is why the Germans prove to be so good at bringing them down. I remember this feeling about the trees because I don't like it and because the trees are alive to me, especially since they must die.

———

So to me the trees are warm bodies. They're certainly warm in the summer sunlight. But cut them down, they're suddenly cold— wounded, killed. That's the difference between a living tree and lumber: lumber is dead wood, regardless of whatever magical thing you turn it into and how beautiful it can be in its afterlife. Mature oaks and maples and shagbark hickories and black walnuts can run four to six and more feet deep and more than a hundred feet tall. Given room to grow, they can spread from tip end of a branch to tip end of a branch at least half of what they are high. Normally, though, crowded in a forest, they narrow and elevate toward the sun. They become more like ladders, ready for climbing. Before power tools, band saws are the means of cutting and handsaws the means of culling away the limbs. (The P. W. Plumly logo includes a script that advertises "Band Saw Hardwood Lumber.")

By hand, forties logging is arduous, risky, painstaking work—it takes time, by hand, to humble a tree, to trim and cut it down: hours sometimes; and trees of a certain size you wouldn't start work on if it was late in the afternoon. The work of the big band saws, in particular, may be a wonder to watch, with a man on each end of a six-to-seven-foot blade that at its widest is at least a foot, tipped with dinosauric teeth. But it's a backbreaking business that requires two men in a sort of awkward dance, in a seesaw, tug-of-war rhythm. It's a rhythm that demands a good number of rests. Yet the Germans turn the dance into something routine, not quite an art, which is to say that they minimize the effort in favor of the achievement. They take their time and save their energy and therefore, ultimately, work faster. And they work through the most dangerous moment of the cutting as intuitively as possible—which I couldn't then have appreciated—since it involves knowing where at some place past halfway through the trunk the point of departure exactly is, depending on the size of inclination . . . the point at which the tree begins to accede.

Unlike my father's usual help, the Germans treat the exhausting job of taking down trees with something like efficiency. The newsreels are constantly referring to "the German war machine"; here—at a ridiculously reduced level—it's the German tree machine: the work done with dispatch but without apparent passion. It's as if the better and quicker they do the job the sooner it can be over—not just the day's job of work but all of it, including the war in Europe and their internment in America. This is how I imagine it now, though at the time the way they worked seemed more like sleight of hand than engineering. Part of it must have had to do with no complaints. The locals were always, it seemed to me, complaining—if it's not the labor, it's the weather; if it's not the extra hour or two, it's the cold food. Perhaps it's because they have no choice, but the Germans waste neither time nor energy being personal. As for complaints, they keep their own counsel. The ratio between the height and weight of a tree, it turns out, *is* personal, individual, and there is no precise predicting how much help it needs in order to make it safely fall. Experience helps, yet the angle of the felling of a tree is predictable only up to where it will likely fall.

Whoever is doing the work—young or old, Virginian or German—an even more dangerous job than cutting is the trimming of the upper-to-lower branches of a standing tree, a one-man exercise, which skill includes strapping onto the tree in a sort of hug as you climb until you reach where you need to be then sawing off, as necessary, various branches and limbs as you walk your way back down. It's possible, I suppose, to saw as you climb, though I don't remember it that way. Only the reverse. The important thing is that you do the trimming with care, so as not to be a victim of your success. A suddenly cut-off branch can sometimes work its own will. The obvious advantage to trimming the tree standing is the possible havoc caused by the width of its branches coming down among other trees.

Even so, I hate, from my head-back-looking-up distance and perspective, watching the limbs free-fall, my eyes half-blinded by the sun. It feels too helter-skelter, chaotic, dangerous, plus the noise and the crashing. Even at five, I can see that trimming, in any form, is denuding, an embarrassment to the nature of things. A great tree without its branching is no longer a tree but a pole rising into dead air. The Germans seem to enjoy this trimming exercise considerably more than the rest of the process, if only because it's more of an individual challenge compared to the tiring, mechanical byplay of the two-man band saw. As trimming can be tricky, my father's older help is happy to watch this enemy take the risks. The Germans seem to like, especially, the standing-tree method.

I should say that it has required some negotiation for me to talk my father into letting me come along on these "German" logging trips. Three or four of my father's regulars, working the woods at a relatively slow pace, is one thing; these new young aliens added into the mix is another. There are, if memory serves—at least at the beginning of the work schedule—a couple of National Guardsmen along, more for comfort than protection, since the Germans appear to be just fine waiting out the war in my grandfather's employment. Their single escape plot seems to be survival, and they couldn't plot any better than here where they are. Forties war movies set in Europe tend to allow escape routes for Allied spies and POWs—Switzerland, Britain, or some French or Dutch Underground hideout. But here, in Virginia, where would you go, and why? Besides, not all eleven of the Germans are in the field at once; it's always the safer number of half.

Besides, the Germans appear to take pride in their work. They are inherently strong, their bodies tightly boned, and their skin, when they take off their shirts in the heat, almost lucent with sweat, proud sweat. Their minds, too, are lucent, and master, in short order, any of the thinking involved in the labor, starting with the procedure of turning trees into logs, then, with the help of pulley-and-chain, moving the logs one at a time into a mass on the flat beds of trucks. Once on board the men use long axe-handle-like poles to direct the different sizes into a more secure place, after which big chains are wrapped around the whole tiered pile and jacked tight. Loading the logs may be even more tricky than cutting the trees. Even so, driving the whole load back down curved mountain roads is the next difficult step, the weight shifting here and there so that you feel it in the cab. And there's always the unloading at the mill, no less dangerous. My father is always the driver, the Germans always together in a separate van.

Why do I remember horses, large plow horses, instead of only tractors or bulldozers? Horses like the horses at my Great Uncle Hub's farm. Memory is a romance with the past or something you bury as deep as or deeper than a hole in the ground. Why go to the trouble of using horses? But I remember them even if they never existed. And sandwiches, scabby old roast beef with butter on white bread and beer and sometimes sausages and apples, from a two-day supply, before somebody brings more, maybe ham sandwiches and milk, and of course water, in big containers, like the milk. The food, regardless, has the faint taste and smell of pine resin and cut wood and dust off the leaves. And then there is the woody coffee, in smaller containers. There would've had to have been grain for the horses, and big water.

————

This is my family's business, the harvesting of trees, the way you harvest wheat or cattle. It's a killing, necessary business. Trees, however, are especially different, not only in their bearing but in the fact that, left alone, they are potentially immortal—immortal as individuals but even more as species and presences to the life on the planet and to human beings in particular, no less so since we climbed down out of them. Bristlecone pines out West can hang on for thousands of years; Great White Oaks in deep forests in the Northeast can last for hundreds. Trees literally stand at the green source of life on the soft earth. As a practical matter they are as essential to our ancestry as to our oxygen supply. And on an entirely different level, they are indelible to the green imagination of the planet. Yet their beauty and necessity are inseparable from their function as timber, even as they represent animate beings, "necessarily sensitive," writes scholar J. G. Frazer, "and the cutting of them down becomes a delicate surgical operation, which must be performed with as tender a regard as possible for the feelings of the sufferers." The Ojibwe believe that cutting down living trees is like the wounding and killing of animals; there is silent pain.

From the contemplative outside, trees appear absolute in their stillness, as if they depend on the wind to animate them. But inside they are moving, within themselves, all the time, ring by ring, season after season. Like all living things they grow from the inside out; and like all living things they are alive with fire.

One Shenandoah summer afternoon I'm wandering around trying to stay out of trouble and trying to find some real shade. Wandering is an exaggeration, since you have to be careful where you sit or stand or walk among the clamor and confusion of who is cutting and who is climbing and at what stage the different jobs are. So you have to walk around with sense. I may be waist-high, maybe a little more. The air is hot and wet with an atmosphere richly mingled with the deep, dry odor of the woods. Sound may be muted, but it carries. The men are talking their business—in German as well as Virginian English—and the saw sound and cut limbs dropping and the scattered sounds of birds are all normal and nothing else, until suddenly a scream, no, a shout of pain that ricochets and echoes, like the snaps of a gun, a sound I think the Germans must be familiar with.

One of the Germans, apparently, has been trimming near the top of an older oak, a large one and one that is oddly top-heavy and bent above an open space removed from the light-seeking straighter trees, those less filled out with foliage. You could see, afterwards, how dry the tree was, the kind lumbermen call a burner, since on its own, in the heat, it can ignite. I remember everyone running in the direction of the shout. By the time I get there it's clear that one of the thinner cut upper branches has blown up into the hand not holding the saw, the German's left hand, and has penetrated the palm with splinters the size of wood spikes, some as large as the sharp ends of pencils. In spite of it all, he has managed, amazingly, to walk his slow way back down on the limbs that are left. My father, who is no doctor, pulls out each of the spikes with care, washing and pouring iodine over the mass of the wounds. Then he wraps the hand in gauze and tape and we call it a day. All this while, except for that first moment of as much surprise as pain, the German soldier has been silent.

FOR GERALD STERN AT NINETY-TWO

At the Great Stern's eightieth birthday party,
at that moment when the meal was ending
and the wine ongoing, Galway stood, with his
bear's hand wrapped around the stem of his glass,
and seemed to be on the verge of a toast, when
instead he lifted his arm as if in victory and asked
all fifty of us to stand with him and recite from
memory "In My Craft or Sullen Art," which we did
as best we could in the "singing light" spreading
all around us. And I have to say I wept, and still
weep when I think about that moment that I can
hardly even speak of now at a distance of some
dozen years—time, "in the mercy of his means,"
refusing to let go of the "secret heart" of poetry.

So I'm on a back road, walking in a direction away
from the viewer, and the question is are those trees
in the upper right hand of the picture Eastern White
pines or simply spruce, the big Blue Spruce of, say,
Vermont or farther up in Maine, near the coast,
because the ground is wet, after a salty rain, and
the sky still dark and drifting, and the feeling is
the feeling of the clarity of being more alone than
ever and being happy, now that there is no death,
only the direction of the future, where daylight
may or may not be ending, and the table may or
may not be set, and someone you love may or
may not be waiting, who until now was outside
the picture, where you, too, have just come from.

WE INSOMNIACS

Like the way Galway Kinnell fell asleep in 1968 in Athens, Ohio,
reading from a wadded-up new poem pulled from his pocket,
started too late at night the night before—
the occasion, exactly, the Ohio Poetry Circuit,
calling for, often, two readings a day, a hundred or so miles apart.
This was an afternoon event, four o'clock,
Body Rags just out, which he also read from.
The new piece was probably from *The Book of Nightmares*,
possibly "Under the Maud Moon," more likely "The Hen Flower,"
which, in the original, begins, "We insomniacs, /
Sprawled / on our faces in the spring / nights . . ."
but later revised—Kinnell was an inveterate reviser—
by dropping the poem's first line,
perhaps a mistake he was now paying for.

I don't remember for sure what the crumpled part of the poem was.
I remember it was a beautiful late October afternoon,
by now four-forty, with the big oaks and maples
on the main campus lawn burning bright outside the windows,
when the poet of the great face and greater soul
allowed himself to lean over from his chair what he had handwritten
(in bed no doubt, under a squeezed under-lit hotel lamp),
and then let fall, in front of his audience, his great head
onto his words, and then, just as sudden, with a snore,
lifted the reading back up to us—the table
he had requested not unlike what we lay
our own great heads on in elementary school for naps.
None of us, as well, had ever slept the night through,
waiting for the dark to disappear.

WAKING

Sometimes, in shadowy first light, it even looks like a horse,
there at the end of the bed like an implement or furniture,
no horn at the center of its forehead,
no wings, only the right number of legs,
and an outline sleek with dew.
Then, long face to face, it looms above your breathing,
the separation of the eyes and its own deep breathing
meant to wake you—the animal standing there at bedside,
rocking back and forth within the stall of itself,
its fist-size nostrils hollowed out,
until, after dawn, it turns its full length around,
circles the bed, as if it's thinking, and walks
over to a wall and puts its head against it.

DEATHBED

Where most of us die, finally quietly, breathless
and alone, regardless of the company, almost the same
way we were born, brought into the world with lights
too bright or the sun burning holes in the air, then
each new night praying our souls to take just in case.
I'm remembering my mother bending over me in order
to try to talk me into sleep but failing until she brings
a radio, with all its lonesome stations and sign-off,
its voices turned so low I'd hear them in my dreams.

Sarcophagi and little wooden shoes spread out among
the stars, tomb-dust and stardust intermingled,
heaven and earth, with memory to sustain us
in the afterlife or the life we've talked ourselves into.
I used to blame my father for the insomnia of the house—
he'd break in at midnight and cook for himself,
too buzzed to know what time it was or even where
he was, then the arguments, long tears, dead silences,
and the hours until the sun and nothing on the radio.

At eighty I've discovered the royal chair, the kind
you sit in to read with wine and hear yourself travel
at the soft end of the day, though right now I'm thinking
end-of-days, the way we fall asleep in the dim afternoon,
without knowing it, in a sort of asleep-at-the-wheel,
and wake up later in a rush, as if we've missed something . . .
Those hours, for instance, that my father took away
or that I gave him back because I loved him.

I think I'll die in a chair. In the ward there'd be those
so wrapped up and infused you'd think they'd already
passed into some place in between, and perhaps,
for the moment, they had—they'd come back smiling,
the slow degrees of pain nearly gone from their faces.
I was lucky, I was only alive, just starting on the journey.
The ward chairs, with windows, were like lounge chairs.
You could fall asleep and not know where you were.

BLUEBIRD

The house was strange, even for a summer house,
cold somehow, the wraparound screened porch
almost cut off by the trees, though the trees, off
and on, would come alive with bluebirds, birds
so tame they would follow on the mountain path
down to the small home lake, *chur-wi, tru-ly,*
chur-wi, tru-ly, over and over, in bird-English.

Had I ever seen a bluebird, so bright a blue?—
a blue easily confused with happiness. I didn't
even know a bluebird was a thrush. I knew
and loved you, that was enough. These blues,
as you called them, were yours: they seemed
to fly in and out of your hands. The lake was one
of those mirror-like lakes. And the house was yours.

In the early days of television, the sometimes blurry black-and-white small-screen days of television, *The Adventures of Ozzie and Harriet* and *Lassie* days, there was another Sunday-safe program called *Zoo Parade*, the first, I think, of its kind on a national basis. Later, the year before John Kennedy's assassination, when TV picture quality had improved with greater clarity and even color, *Zoo Parade* would evolve into *Mutual of Omaha's Wild Kingdom*. Both were considered to be "nature" programming. And both were hosted by the St. Louis Zoo's eventual director Marlin Perkins, a senior-looking, reassuring Missourian.

Wild Kingdom, as much as possible, tried to be on location, but more often than not the show started out at the zoo itself, believed to be, at the time—including the nineteen fifties—one of the most thought-out of such places, with larger open sections devoted to like-minded flight animals as well as air-controlled "houses" for reptiles and big cats and monkeys. The walking-plan of it all, too, allowed for space and interest—winding lanes and people-friendly sitting areas, enough that you could get a little lost among the crowds.

She liked to tell the story, with the distance of amusement, of her abandonment at the zoo, but tell it also as a way to dispel it, take away its power. The more often the telling the less it seemed to hurt—that, at least, was the idea. The Sugarbakers live in Jefferson City, the state capital, a little over a hundred miles west from St. Louis. One spring Sunday, after nine o'clock church (Dutch Reformist translated into Church of Christ), the family all pile into one of their two vintage Rolls Royces and head for St. Louis and the Marlin Perkins zoo. There will ultimately be ten children, six girls, four boys, while at the moment there are six, maybe seven—ranging from early adolescence to preschool—and at a kindergarten five she is in the middle.

Even at a mixed-size six or so, along with two parents, there are enough Sugarbaker bodies to fill, each Sunday, a front-row pew. Yet managing to fit into one capacious Rolls must be a different kind of physical problem. I used to ask her if, in fact, they drove to St. Louis that day in both big cars, mother and father driving; but, no, she'd insist, there was just the one, packed tight, all in their church-best.

She is already the outsider, the artist among a family of scientists, mainly medical. She will start out as a painter, then a poet, though who can tell who'll turn out to be what when you look at a 1955 family photograph, where she stands more or less in the middle, her mother holding up one end with a baby in her arms. More often than should be, she's called by one of her sister's names, a sister standing on either side of her in the picture.

Is it July or a hot August afternoon when they arrive at the zoo? They must be a sight, the two tall, distinguished-looking parents, with their well-dressed brood—including the baby in a carriage—following along, on parade. Indeed, as she remembers it, as they trail from exhibit to exhibit, they appear to be also on display, which is why—and this is my own speculation after a third or fourth hearing—she begins to feel an especial empathy for the animals, since the Sugarbakers—in their good clothes—must suddenly seem exotic, like flowers, like flowers, as Eliot says, that have the look of flowers that are looked at. They take their time, they pay attention; this is a learning experience.

rls, four boys, while at the moment there are six, maybe
—ranging from early adolescence to preschool—and at a
rgarten five she is in the middle.

t a mixed-size six or so, along with two parents, there are
h Sugarbaker bodies to fill, each Sunday, a front-row pew.
naging to fit into one capacious Rolls must be a different
physical problem. I used to ask her if, in fact, they drove
ouis that day in both big cars, mother and father driving;
she'd insist, there was just the one, packed tight, all in
urch-best.

ready the outsider, the artist among a family of
s, mainly medical. She will start out as a painter, then
hough who can tell who'll turn out to be what when
at a 1955 family photograph, where she stands more or
e middle, her mother holding up one end with a baby
ns. More often than should be, she's called by one of
s names, a sister standing on either side of her in the

a hot August afternoon when they arrive at the zoo?
be a sight, the two tall, distinguished-looking parents,
vell-dressed brood—including the baby in a carriage—
ong, on parade. Indeed, as she remembers it, as they
xhibit to exhibit, they appear to be also on display,
y—and this is my own speculation after a third or
ng—she begins to feel an especial empathy for the
e the Sugarbakers—in their good clothes—must
m exotic, like flowers, like flowers, as Eliot says, that
of flowers that are looked at. They take their time,
tion; this is a learning experience.

I think I'll die in a chair. In the ward there'd be those
so wrapped up and infused you'd think they'd already
passed into some place in between, and perhaps,
for the moment, they had—they'd come back smiling,
the slow degrees of pain nearly gone from their faces.
I was lucky, I was only alive, just starting on the journey.
The ward chairs, with windows, were like lounge chairs.
You could fall asleep and not know where you were.

The house was strange, even for a summer house,
cold somehow, the wraparound screened porch
almost cut off by the trees, though the trees, off
and on, would come alive with bluebirds, birds
so tame they would follow on the mountain path
down to the small home lake, *chur-wi, tru-ly,*
chur-wi, tru-ly, over and over, in bird-English.

Had I ever seen a bluebird, so bright a blue?—
a blue easily confused with happiness. I didn't
even know a bluebird was a thrush. I knew
and loved you, that was enough. These blues,
as you called them, were yours: they seemed
to fly in and out of your hands. The lake was one
of those mirror-like lakes. And the house was yours.

In the early days of television, the sometime
white small-screen days of television, *The A*
Harriet and *Lassie* days, there was another
called *Zoo Parade*, the first, I think, of its
Later, the year before John Kennedy's assa
picture quality had improved with greate
Zoo Parade would evolve into *Mutual of*
Both were considered to be "nature" pro
were hosted by the St. Louis Zoo's even
Perkins, a senior-looking, reassuring M

Wild Kingdom, as much as possible, tr
more often than not the show started
to be, at the time—including the nin
thought-out of such places, with lar
like-minded flight animals as well
reptiles and big cats and monkeys.
allowed for space and interest—wi
sitting areas, enough that you cou
crowds.

She liked to tell the story, with t
abandonment at the zoo, but te
away its power. The more often
hurt—that, at least, was the id
City, the state capital, a little
St. Louis. One spring Sunday
Reformist translated into Ch
into one of their two vintag
and the Marlin Perkins zoo

six g
sever
kinde

Even
enoug
Yet ma
kind o
to St. L
but, no
their ch

She is al
scientist
a poet, tl
you look
less in th
in her arr
her sister
picture.

Is it July o
They must
with their
following a
trail from e
which is wl
fourth hear
animals, sin
suddenly see
have the look
they pay atter

At a school-age five, she feels sorry for these animal captives, there are so many of them, so many kinds. She obviously identifies with them—in both their capture and their anonymity, regardless of whether or not they're named. Some of the animals yawn, a deep death yawn of boredom; some pace around in circles as if to enlarge the numbing space; some simply stare out through the bars or glass as if they're blind. The snakes seem to be semiconscious or asleep. This is lost life, she thinks. The zoo is a prison.

This last point is a point of emphasis.

The day passes off and on, with snacks and ice cream and rests in between, until near closing time and the closing bell. It's summer, so the light lasts longer. The Sugarbakers leave the zoo probably around 6:00, maybe later, with the hope of beating the worst of the Sunday traffic. Everyone is tired and cranky and in a hurry to get home, a two-hour-plus drive ahead of them. They pile back into the big car sort of here and there, the baby and one or two of the smallest Sugarbakers in the front with the parents. Halfway home, in the large, crowded backseat, no Deborah.

Now the light is beginning to fail, turn dusky. Dr. Sugarbaker turns the car around, turns the headlights on, and starts back, an hour, at least, away.

Forgetting her name is one thing, forgetting her altogether is another. Each time she's told the story she's remembered to link the two. And each time, the interlude between being left and being found changes in detail. The outlines, though, are clear. She must have wandered awhile, looking for her family; someone must have noticed her. She must be crying, but softly, so as not to draw attention. The zoo was closing, the evening coming down. Rather soon she would have been taken to lost-and-found, so to speak, and quizzed. There were surely big tears by now and broken answers. No one would have been at home even if the authorities had had a phone number. She was now a sort of prisoner too, captive of an isolation.

What to do with her? Time is passing. Finally her parents arrive, though it could have been a complication getting back onto the zoo grounds—it had been awhile since the early Sunday closing. No harm done, we like to say. Or as the mother often summed up trouble: nobody died.

But abandonment doesn't go away, whether voluntary or involuntary. She once told me that under an analyst's hypnosis she could see herself back down there in that moment bumping into a table that was just head-high, in a room like an office with all kinds of zoo paraphernalia. I think she dreamed the scene in the office on a regular basis.

This one time, in my experience, she cried. It's not hard to imagine, at the depth of the heart, what a five-year-old from a large family must have felt now suddenly alone, anonymous among strangers in a night-strange place and the night sounds looming from the animal cages. The story of the imagination is about such memory, however pure or compiled from different sources. When she repeated the narrative of the moment in the zoo office, rescued first from the sleep of hypnosis, then retold as remembered, she must have rubbed the place on her forehead where she hit the table.

THE WARD

The ones with wigs enter the sterile space
with their eyes cast down, the ones with
kerchiefs focus on the air straight ahead
of them—I still have my hair, though only in
a sort of slow-growth way, like frost on a stone.
The lounge-like chairs are lined up facing
the wall-to-ceiling windows, if not for
the view then for the fantasy of freedom,
like deck chairs, with wool blankets, only
a few feet from the rail and the great Atlantic.

Some of us read or listen through earbuds
to self-help books or the music of the spheres,
some simply talk out loud to mitigate
the silence and the kindness of the nurses.
We are all alive, regardless, God save us.
No one, however, speaks to his/her neighbor.
Whatever's in the meds is Keatsian,
"dull opiate to the drains" and always
"one minute past" whatever we think time is.
All this, whatever else it is, is health.

How many kinds of cancer are there?—
as many as there are cells, beginning
with the sperm and ovum, shaped through
the microscope to look like something
floating death miles deeper in the sea.
The heart is a machine, but this is different:
a snake around the heart, the worm inside
the lung, the eel electric through the journey

of the colon: outside the windows, the cloud
cells forming and reforming like everything

inside us. And everything is cancer.
Everyone is cancer. The woman in pajamas
on one side of me, the man in a gown on
the other . . . I can see the girl in the striped
bandanna asking for water, for another
blanket, for the needle, once again, to be
checked on—I can see myself as nothing but
the flow from the purity of chemistry in the bag
above me, finding its way through the city
that I was into the open country of my body.

ALZHEIMER'S

I can still look down the middle of Five Shillings
to where the trees diminish at far Mill Pond
     and see it will be later the longer their distance.
And better now that it's December,
the leaves almost gone, the trimmed elm-like branching
     lifting higher toward the sun.
I used to think that memory was like hallways
at my Township Elementary School,
     with floor-to-ceiling windows at each end,
     the undulant oak floors so polished as to bless you,
each graduated open classroom a welcoming through time.
     The mind loves metaphor, especially
     the odd-or-even ends of things, though looking down
the street at how the winter ornamentals line up
     like the past may not always satisfy imagination,
     while in the spoil of summer, in a sequence
of green moments, they may suggest the present more alive,
     it's the long view, in the long run, that matters.
Including the nice houses that like the trees
along the street also diminish in perspective,
     like those who live inside them, like us.
Like the friendly neighbor walking toward the camera
who gets lost in all the shadow and bright detail,
     and if we could remember her young face,
     first name, let alone her heart, that might or might not
be enough to justify my childhood hallway poetry,
     its classrooms and star windows,
     and the patience with which we'd stand in line
after a practice fire alarm, regardless of the season,
     then file back in to climb back up the worn
     but certain stairs to where the sunlight was waiting.

NIGHT PASTORALS

1

Real time is when a thing happens but you're only aware that it really happened later. I was already in trouble with multiple myeloma that was attacking my kidneys—on my right side. Then came the pneumonia—on my left, so severe that the two main lung doctors suggested to my wife that she might have to let me go.

She said no. If anything, she said, no, I would die in my own bed. And I would be given the chance to finish a last book, regardless of the odds. It's as if she waved her hand, since the next morning I rose with enough life left in me to go on.

It is no news to say that we die in our shadows, those selves that seem to perpetually occupy the space next to us. In reality, in death we slip away into silence, without, I'll bet, the least past of a dream. I don't remember dying, nor, in any ordinary sense, living again. I didn't seem to be there, among the winding sheets of the hospital linen, then again I was. I'd slipped, then slipped back.

I'm reminded that as a child, late at night, I loved to hear the adults talking—their quiet resonance put me to sleep. My small moment with the other side was like that.

2

When I was nine we moved back to Ohio, where my father proceeded to build us a house. He did it mostly himself, so it took a while, a year. We stayed at my grandmother's, where my sister slept upstairs in a big sort of glamorous wooden double bed that smelled of the mothballs kept in the winter drawers to protect the wool. Right outside the window by the bed was a great catalpa stationed in front of the front porch roof—the two of us would sit in the summer late into the night on that roof and toss off into the street the black leathery cigars the tree dropped like leaves.

I slept downstairs on the daybed in the dining room. My parents had their own bedroom space next to my sister's. Grandma Ruth and her second husband's bedroom smelled of real cigars and the odor of the ambivalence of old ladies. Ruth was special that way.

I've always been a light sleeper, perhaps in part because of a tiresome requirement that children should go to bed early, a rule I broke consistently once we moved into our new drafty house out in the country. Anyway there I was, a child, on my daybed, usually at twilight, staring at the ceiling or more commonly listening.

I loved listening to the residual radio, a big Philco, whose voice rode over the voices of the adults like atop a wave. It came from the front room, just adjacent to the dining room, where my grandmother sat each evening at the dining table listening too, coming down from her very busy day.

3

Ruth was a registered nurse, also a kind of "Rosie the Riveter," both of which callings were vital during the war. Some days, doubtless, she filled both roles. Like me, she liked listening from a distance, sitting at the long dining table smoking, legs crossed, one leg in motion over the other. She smoked fast and seemed to listen within her own blue cloud.

I think she listened like me, in a sliding dream way. For me, the low tones of the radio and the quiet punctuation of whoever was in the living room trying to talk quietly made the drift toward sleep that much easier.

For my grandmother I think it all helped her sort out the day and separate this from that. Some evenings she still had on her nurse's uniform, some her French Oil work outfit. Either way she always wore a red kerchief around a wrist and hummed to herself. I guess she eventually joined the group.

4

Ruth's father was a one-room schoolteacher for more than fifty years. I knew him—he lived to be ninety-eight and lived with us at his daughter's South Downing house for as long as I can remember. He had his own ancient room, small but perfect. He was a formal person and dressed for teaching every morning, so that aging into the twilight he looked like the past. You might say he wore the wool and flannel textures of disappearance. He always seemed to me to be in two worlds at once: perhaps one of them death. Lying like a ghost in a hospital bed night after night, week after week, trying not to die again, I began to fix on my memory of him.

At ninety-eight, in the nineteen forties, it meant, for one thing, that William DeBrae was born around 1850, maybe before. I'd have to look at his stone again. His age meant a lot of things. For one, it meant that little Covington, Ohio, the once-home of the country schoolhouse, is only a few miles from Piqua, where we all lived; it meant that my great-grandfather, by choice, had to bike there, weather in, weather out.

I remember the bicycle clips around his upper ankles. I remember most his bicycle itself, which he bought from the Wright Brothers, in Dayton, and which he kept in loving condition, like his room, even when he got too old to navigate it. We're talking mid-nineteenth century and on into the air age. You enter, in your mind, in the white darkness of a hospital, half here, half there, all kinds of corridors of time.

So I'm thinking that William DeBrae was about ten when the Civil War broke out, which means he was old enough to know any leftover crutch-walking failing antediluvian veterans of the Revolutionary War, which ended in 1783. Lying there, awake with the nurses, after some middle-of-the-night treatment, I could walk myself back there and think it real. Think it something, anyway.

5

"Vigil strange"—writes Whitman in *Drum-Taps*, in 1865—"I kept on the field one night; / When you my son and my comrade dropt at my side that day, / One look I but gave which your dear eyes return'd with a look I shall never forget . . ." You get lost in consciousness when day turns to night and back again and you see into different eyes and the solution you're floating in lets you ride in deeper, higher silence. You could fall into the heart of your grave and not know it, which I believe I did when those lung doctors thought they heard me break a last breath.

No wonder Whitman loves "the passing of blood and air through my lungs, / The sniff of green leaves and dry leaves, and of the shore and dark-color'd sea-rocks, and of hay in the barn." No wonder he loves the "spears" and little knives of the leaves of grass. The white sleepless abyss of the hospital bed just goes down and down, like a work-boat without rest.

6

Late, very late, you could hear in a far hallway someone crying or crying out—to what hope of help, who knew. There was resonance to the voices, primary, animal sounds. The hallways magnified the volume.

My greater problem, on my right side, was that the myeloma was so multiple it was now after my kidneys—and was succeeding in what in medical parlance is called "late-stage renal disease." I'd already been in this indifferent bed for two pneumonia weeks—or was it longer?—though I felt no pain, which was in itself strange.

Coming up would be the new long hours of kidney dialysis, red blood cells the color of deep maple. Same bed, but moved to the wider realm of company.

7

So, more weeks of endless sleepless nights, nailed to the cross, the spirit. Not that I needed the company. Nurses, in pale starched blue and white, seemed to come and go in military tattoo, no matter where they put me. And in the dawn light of each gray morning, doctors showing up, like judges.

I'm thinking again of how much all the attention kept me awake,
at a distance from dying.

8

Close your eyes for too long and you can be gone. We thought the
dream was a dream: we thought this later.

Nothing in nature loves us. The flowers, says Eliot, merely have
the look of flowers that are looked at. But they are beautiful,
especially wild. And wild they won't last.

And I'm thinking, lying there, in a rare moment, "struck," it
seems, "from the float forever held in solution," wondering
why she chose to try to fly—impulse, I'm sure, the way she did
everything. Climbing the great stadium stairs, then looking
down into the fifty-year-old heart of the air, listening to a kind of
calling—her parents, her children, poetry itself—the wish must
have been overwhelming.

9

If I ever walk again . . .

10

Bread of the body, wine of the blood—one bread, one blood.
Just in that one small hospital, as one nurse referred to it, all our
bodies linked as if holding hands: the city of my hand.

When I was angry and spoke in anger as a child and told my mother how much I hated her, she'd help me pack and fix a lunch to carry on my bike as far as daylight would take me. Not far.

There was a bridge, hardly a bridge at all, where I'd slip under and spend the hour or more thinking through the nothing that had brought me there. Sometimes it rained, sometimes the sun poured a shadow.

11

If you're talking I'm listening. One nurse, one deep well of the night, spoke of joy, the luck of the pocket, the blue marble there. She looked right at me as if she knew me.

Lying there, flat as a field, I was nothing but nature, though I was aware—some nights more than others—of its distances.

JESUS WEPT.

The shortest sentence, I believe, in the New Testament.
Having to do with the raising of Lazarus, and no less
the crucifixion of Jesus himself once the Pharisees
realize the power of a voice that can call forth the dead.
Jesus seems to be identifying with this brother of Martha
and Mary, with in fact the whole weeping community.
Take away the stone, Lazarus come forth, and he that was
dead came forth, bound hand and foot with graveclothes;
and his face was bound about with a napkin. *Loose him
and let him go.*

       Then why am I now weeping all the time,
who does not want to be called forth, let alone wrapped
in white? I believe in death, I believe in the last tree I will
ever see, perhaps with wind in it just as it's turning color.
I believe in my friends' weeping and in the terrible sorrow
of my wife, but why, on this side of things, with death still
only a small secret moving inside me, am I so hurt with pity
for myself, as if, one by one, anything I touch will disappear,
whatever I see deeply will suddenly become invisible to me?

Is it the loneliness, the body gone, the table and the chair
and the bowl that had the heartless flowers floating in it?
So that all that is left is whatever a soul is as your stand-in?
When I was alive I remember feeling myself beside myself
sometimes, as if I'd already passed to somewhere else and
for that moment was in two places at once, no place and
a place without me: a moment, I suppose, so lonely it was
enough to make you weep, though not so much then but
later when the absence stayed with you and became you.

AT NIGHT

When did I know that I'd have to carry it around
in order to have it when I need it, say in a pocket,

the dark itself not dark enough but needing to be
added to, handful by handful if necessary, until

the way my mother would sit all night in a room
without the lights, smoking, until she disappeared?

Where would she go, because I would go there.
In the morning, nothing but a blanket and all her

absence and the feeling in the air of happiness.
And so much loneliness, a kind of purity of being

and emptiness, no one you are or could ever be,
my mother like another me in another life, gone

where I will go, night now likely dark enough
I can be alone as I've never been alone before.

Strange what you remember. When I think of my mother the
first thing I think of is her feet, her flat duck feet, with their
bunions and calluses and size-whatever complaints; with their
deep bottom crisscross lines, like dry rivers, lining every which
way, as if to tell her fortune. Not that her feet were immediately-
looking odd or outsized, only that in her youth she'd tried, like a
Cinderella sister, to squeeze them into shoes that didn't fit, shoes
on sale or that had some special claim to beauty. At least this
was her story. It was the Depression, she'd say, as if poverty had
anything to do with it, which, as I imagine the subtlety of poverty,
its depravations and denials, may be partly true.

As she got older her feet took on further distortion—they didn't
seem to belong to the nice legs and mother body above them.
They'd sometimes look attached, from another time, peasant feet,
field-worker from a painting. I'm probably exaggerating, but they
seemed, at times, to tread rather than simply walk the ground.
And it's not as if she didn't try to correct the disparity, so that the
different thing is the degree to which she cared for them: the salt
baths, the medicinal creams, the delicate foot files, the inserts to
shoes, the high heels relieved with flats.

At home, cooking, doing laundry or housework, she wore
slippers that fit like old gloves, which is to say she might as well
have been barefoot, except for the fact that the slippers tended
to slap the floor while her feet on their own were silent. Once
a week she saw what she called her foot doctor, Dr. Schucutt—
Shoe-Cut, I called him. I met him once, waiting in the waiting
room. He was small and bent a bit—from bending over to
perform his examinations, I thought, like a shoe salesman or a

cobbler. My mother looked forward to these visits, both because they gave her some relief and because—now that I think about it—they were sensual experiences: the little surgeries, the hand-handling, the ministering of medicines, the mere intimate attentions, the feet as something utterly personal.

I have my mother's feet, pancake feet. Our feet, after all, are the platforms of our being and the first parts of our bodies the ancients paid caring and public attention to, especially in welcoming visitors. Think of the thousands of years and the millions of miles that our feet have carried us on the footpaths and across the thresholds. No wonder we've anointed them with oil and blessed their travel, though it's unlikely that my mother, on her best day, could have covered a walking mile.

Yet those feet were the most human part of her, the most vulnerable and reassuring. As a small child I loved touching them, particularly the calluses, which were, in imagination, like Grandpappy Lyn's wen—ugly, otherworldly, magical. I think there were moments when she too loved those feet, loved them the way we come to accept our flaws as essential to our identities. I once compared the warmth and character of my mother's feet to a "bricklayer's hands," and those hands, I realize now, are my father's hands.

———

That's the part of his body I remember most, those large hard hands, that could squeeze the juice from an apple. In his prime, my father was six feet, weighed 200 or so pounds, and had a thirty-two-inch waist. He had a laborer's hands, almost as callused as my mother's feet. To watch him with an axe or hammer, the way his right hand swallowed the handle, was to be impressed. To watch him lift a tray of bricks and carry it up a ladder or hold a shovel or move an anvil cradled between his arms, his hands in fists . . .

When he stopped working in the woods he turned to welding, mostly because by then we'd left Virginia for Ohio, and left nature for industry, though the farmer in him never left him. Perhaps he saw some artistry in drawing a seam of soft hot metal in order to heal a rift. He looked ominous in the welder's mask, though at both French Oil and Dupps he was soon promoted out of the welder's chair and mask to foreman.

Some of my happiest times with him were helping him build our half-built house and watching him use those hands. For him it was an after-work and weekend job, for me an after-school fantasy. I was nine. He had two workmen from work to fill out with the extras, cheap labor for the least skilled of the digging of foundations and measuring off of rooms and mixing hod and generally holding things together. I sort of carried bits and pieces and stayed out of the way and played the spy. The three of them poured the concrete floors, but it was my father who laid the brick and leveled its flat-face surfaces and angles, sometimes better than other times.

It was my father who shaped the shape of the roof, his big raw hands handling the two-by-sixes as if they were mere lumber, which, of course they were—the helper workmen at each end of the longer pieces, just like those years ago in the woods. We were always working against the clock, which is to say the weather, since our work hours were always up against sunset and the rain and, finally, the snow. The first year the house was enough of a shell we could work inside on walls and windows and doors, none of which seemed quite right, as if my father's hands lacked the subtlety of the square.

The thing is that my father was a sober house-builder, then a drunk after dark, when he would disappear—as far as I knew—until the next morning, usually late for his regular foreman's job. He finally lost his position at French Oil for being late at least a hundred too many times, but by then we'd pretty well closed on finishing our half-finished house.

It sat in the countryside on Garbry Road just outside Piqua, Ohio, practically in the middle of a cornfield. It ultimately turned out to be a small farmhouse, with an added small barn and a couple of outbuildings. When I'd come back summer from college I'd find different additions and combinations of domesticity that might include a couple of useless horses, a donkey, chickens, a half-dozen white-faced Herefords, a pen of youngish pigs, whatever. My father always wept sending off the cattle to slaughter. And he seemed just as close to tears each evening talking to his pigs, whom he petted on their pink heads with great care with his great hands.

CREPUSCULAR

That late poem by Housman, Roman numeral
XVI, where the sun is rising "beautiful to sight"
and falling "into the west away," where "like a bird
set free," it soars "from the eastern sea," only
to end up stained with blood "ensanguining the skies"
before it becomes "hopeless under ground"—

that poem whose middle stanza, between the rising
and the falling, takes the pledge that the poet,
on this day, "shall be strong," and "no more . . . yield
to wrong," indeed "shall squander life no more"
and keep this "vow / I never kept before"—
that poem of "days lost, I know not how,"

that seems so perfect, personal, and vulnerable,
so English in its resignation and elegant in execution,
like that poem that finds a home at last in Larkin,
an aubade of the end, where he's awake in
"soundless dark," standing at "the curtain-edges"
waiting for industrial dawn to break open in a room

of "total emptiness for ever"; or like Hardy's
"Neutral Tones," where the "God-curst sun" is
winter "white"; or Dickinson's "Twilight long begun . . .
Sequestered Afternoon," where "The Dusk drew"
early on—after "The Morning foreign shone";
or that final "still dark" stairway poem by Bishop,

in her last, *Geography III*, where she's exhausted
"Five Flights Up" from climbing one more step,

just one more step from the "Enormous morning"
and its "ponderous, meticulous" / "gray light streaking
each bare branch, / each single twig, along one side, /
making another tree, of glassy veins"; or like "Epilogue,"

by Lowell, who, underneath the "plot and rhyme"
of drugs, is always asking "why not say what happened"
since we're "poor passing facts," facts, he says, that give
"the grace of accuracy," even if they're "threadbare"
in the eye, facts like the kind "Vermeer gave to the sun's
illumination / stealing like the tide across a map /

to his girl solid with yearning"—the sun itself ending
the day with longing, "not further to be found,"
as Housman puts it, except again and again, "past touch
and sight and sound" only to emerge in the new day
dawning "heightened from life, / yet paralyzed by fact"
as "something imagined, not recalled" (Lowell).

AS YOU LEAVE THE ROOM

Wallace Stevens at Harvard reading to
his eight readers, who drift, one at a time,
out of the room, until I'm the only
audience left, and even I have doubts
that this fat man in a suit is really
real or that when I also leave the room
he will care or even know I was here.

As I leave the room, as I leave the room,
as I walk into the hall where the future
has gathered, I wonder how long Stevens
will be standing there, reading himself
to himself, " . . . a skeleton out of its cabinet . . . "
having lived, he fears, " . . . a skeleton's life,
/ As a disbeliever in reality, // A countryman

of all the bones in the world," part of an
ongoing conversation with imagination,
"part of / An appreciation of a reality
// And thus an elevation," like the real
possibility of a snowman in January. As
I leave the room, it's as if he's only talking
to himself "About the mind as never satisfied."

"The river is moving. / The blackbird must
be flying." As I leave the room, as I enter
my own mind, I'm wondering who is more
alone, the fat man in the suit or the bones
inside the fat man or the audience of one,
or is the loneliness of poetry the point,
since that is who we are, what we have.

HOUSE

Door frames off the square, the inside
sweating tile-brick walls uncovered,
the checkerboard linoleum floors tilted
toward infinity or at least in the direction
of my northern bedroom window, which
in winter is half-frozen with ice thick
enough some mornings to draw on
with a fingernail, while in the dust of
summer the heat though everywhere
fills up the sunburned space with what
my sister calls the angels, who live also
in the attic, no less famous for its stars
and star-like rain that sometimes slips
on through the ceiling into the shy air.

A man standing before his children with
nothing in his hands, the angst coming
down like air the weight of gravity through
the whole length of his body, a lifetime
of falling and slow settling like night fog
or soft rain, as if there were a lake inside
him and above that the cloud-float of
a mind, until a day, like now, the water
rises to the limits of its form: and
it does no good to say that fathers are
the fathers of their own misery, it does
no good to take it all to heart, when
all he is doing is standing there, alone,
in silence, disappearing into himself.

THE WINTER BEACH AT SANDERLING

The "wolves in the waves" driving or being driven
inside the rain, which is one sort of day to be alone
in, then again the beach mile either way disappearing
into the thinness of the air, dead detail of the gone world
from the night before—probably an eaten-out barrel
or two, traps and lines of netting, lumber and almost
carcasses and scored horseshoe shells—brought home
from who knows where, then someone with a dog
making a single shadow out of an idea of sun: each
day rising and thinking I died for some kind of beauty,
standing in the morning on the height of my deck,
trying to wake up, nothing but my eyes to go by—
how dark down does the water go before the tide—
I the god of starfish fallen, the flounder's whiter bones.

WITH WEATHER

All day you watch the frost flare
into each end point of the star.
The cold is like glass on your skin.
You know if you sit here long enough
how brittle the body becomes.
Even the paling evening is on two sides.
But you sit in the sun half, half sun,
the lie in your lap, filling your face.
You're like a man in love with something—
some word, a gesture, the one line of light
lost among a line of trees, a man in a chair
watching it starting to rain a little and snow.
You could get up and join the snow.
You could move to a warmer window.
You could move to the middle of the room.
You could get up and turn on the light.
You could sit here alone

NOTES

Notes are listed by poem in order of appearance, and then by page number.

PLANET

22   The phrase "the resurrection of the wheat" comes from Walt Whitman's poem "This Compost."

TRAVEL & LEISURE

28–29   The Ernest Hemingway phrases are from *A Moveable Feast*.

30   John Keats' phrase about his "death warrant" comes from Charles Brown's account of Keats' illness in "Life of John Keats," *The Keats Circle: Letters and Papers, 1816–1878*.

30   The passage beginning "Hampstead Heath / was the common" is from *Michelin Green Guide London*.

30–31   Samuel Taylor Coleridge's comment about meeting Keats on Hampstead Heath is from his *Specimens of the Table Talk of Samuel Taylor Coleridge*.

31   The Henry James passage that begins "Beauty is no compensation" comes from the essay "Roman Rides" in his *Italian Hours*.

32   Henry Wadsworth Longfellow's phrase "white swan of cities" is from his poem "Venice."

32   William Dean Howells' comment about the "summer-delight of other lands" comes from his *Venetian Life*.

32   Charles Dickens' passage about "looking down upon the Grand Canal" is taken from an 1844 letter that Dickens sent to John Forster.

35   William Hazlitt is referring to the painter J. M. W. Turner in his comment that the artist "delights to go back to the first chaos of the world." This comment appears in his book *The Round Table: A Collection of Essays on Literature, Men, and Manners*.

35   Walt Whitman's two phrases come from his poem "To a Locomotive in Winter."

36   Robert Lowell's comments about the painter John Constable are from his poem "Painter."

36   The original use by John Constable of the phrase "the *chiaroscuro* of nature" was around 1832, when he issued a collection of twenty-two images—plates of his own paintings engraved in mezzotint by David Lucas. In 1833, the second edition carried the overall title *Various subjects of Landscape, characteristic of English Scenery, principally intended to mark the Phenomena of the Chiar'Oscuro of Nature*.

GERMANS

57   The passage about trees from J. G. Frazer is taken from *The Golden Bough*.

FOR GERALD STERN AT NINETY-TWO

59   The three phrases are from Dylan Thomas' poetry; "singing light" and the "secret heart" of poetry are from

"In My Craft or Sullen Art," while "in the mercy of his means" comes from "Fern Hill."

WE INSOMNIACS

60   Galway Kinnell's passage beginning "Sprawled / on our faces" comes from "The Hen Flower" section of *The Book of Nightmares*.

ONE OF TEN

66   The paraphrase about flowers from T. S. Eliot is from section one of "Burnt Norton" in *Four Quartets*.

THE WARD

69   The John Keats phrases, "dull opiate to the drains" and "one minute past," are from his poem "Ode to a Nightingale."

NIGHT PASTORALS

75   Walt Whitman's passage beginning "Vigil strange" comprises the first three lines of his poem "Vigil Strange I Kept on the Field one Night."

76   The passage beginning "the passing of blood and air through my lungs" is from the second section of Walt Whitman's "Song of Myself."

77   The paraphrase about flowers from T. S. Eliot is from section one of "Burnt Norton" in *Four Quartets*.

CREPUSCULAR

85–86 A. E. Housman's short phrases are from his poem "How clear, how lovely bright," which appears as section XVI in *More Poems*.

85   Philip Larkin's phrases come from his poem "Aubade."

85   Thomas Hardy's phrases are from his poem "Neutral Tones."

85   Emily Dickinson's passages beginning with "Twilight long begun" come from her poem referred to by the title "As imperceptibly as Grief" or identified as #935 in R. W. Franklin's numbering.

85–86 Elizabeth Bishop's poem "Five Flights Up" is the source for the lines quoted here.

86   Robert Lowell's lines quoted here are from his poem "Epilogue."

AS YOU LEAVE THE ROOM

87   Most of the quoted lines are from Wallace Stevens's poem "As You Leave the Room," while the two lines beginning "The river is moving" come from his "Thirteen Ways of Looking at a Blackbird."

THE WINTER BEACH AT SANDERLING

89   The poem commences with a quoted phrase, "wolves in the waves," which likely derives from a kenning in *Beowulf*, in which Grendel's mother is referred to as "wolf-of-the-waves."

PERMISSIONS ACKNOWLEDGMENTS

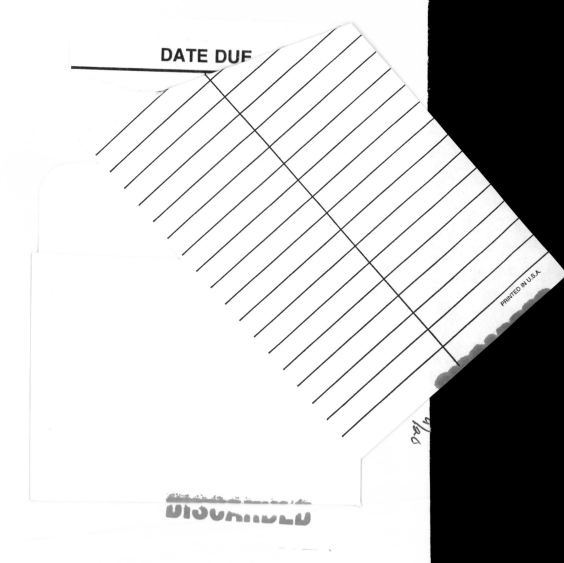

DATE DUE

PRINTED IN U.S.A.